# One Night We Will No Longer Bear the Ocean

Poems

Anton Yakovlev

ELJ Editions, Ltd. is committed to publishing works of quality and integrity. In that spirit, we are proud to offer this poetry collection to our readers. Names, characters, places, and incidents either are the product of the author's imagination or are used fictitiously, and any resemblance to actual persons, living or dead, business establishments, events, or locales is entirely coincidental.

ISBN: 978-1-942004-71-4

Library of Congress Control Number: 2024937233

Cover Design by Shay Culligan

Redacted Books, an imprint of ELJ Editions

ELJ Editions, Ltd.
P.O. Box 815
Washingtonville, NY 10992

www.elj-editions.com

# Praise for *One Night We Will No Longer Bear the Ocean*

"Reading this book had a radical effect on me: it is poetry that tears off the bandage over a wounded heart, a return to the source of lyric poetry. At the same time, it sets off the almost forgotten flame of what was once unapologetically poetry. In so doing, history, geography and architecture exist as the ragged costumes in an ongoing human tragedy. Anton Yakovlev is an immensely talented poet who has the courage to go lucidly against the grain to what hurts. He drafts history and terror to his pain: 'all human history smells like boots' and 'If guillotines could sing, would they sing in your voice?' This 'you' owns the cosmic cold: 'no matter how much you sang / your teeth were Stonehenge / or typewriter keys.' What incredible gift to the 'you' that has set this poetry in motion!"

—Andrei Codrescu, author of *So Recently Rent a World: New and Selected Poems*

"One of the most original voices in contemporary poetry, Anton Yakovlev has given us a dissonant hymn to unrequited love that is as surprising as it is unsentimental. In *One Night We Will No Longer Bear the Ocean*, he tracks the landscape of a years-long relationship, its roots in trauma, its symphonies and missed connections—'we argue and we clutch'—played out against a backdrop featuring, in turn, Edward Snowden, Laika the ill-fated Sputnik dog, 'dangerous books getting burned in the most beautiful square.' Devastatingly precise, funny, and intensely human, these poems will leave you changed."

—Theresa Burns, author of *Design*

"How to write a poem if you're Anton Yakovlev: 1. Dive off Dali's waxed mustache into The Land of Melted Watches. 2. Immediately transform into Alice's White Rabbit. 3. Race past Brodsky snooping for Véronique's red velvet armchair in every Trotskyist cafeteria in the city. 4. Read the future in counterfeit Tarot cards. 5. Your hand reaches into the bonfire seconds before it fades. Now the poem is done. BUT IS IT?! Not if you're our man Yakovlev, whose imagery machine guns every so-called word. Yet, hidden in this avalanche is a bravura confluence of shimmering imagery from which humanity emerges, an endangered species, searching for love."

—Bob Holman, creator of *The United States of Poetry*

## Editor's Note

Dear Reader,

When I created the Redacted Books Series for ELJ Editions, in collaboration with Ariana Den Bleyker, my idea was to bring voice to poets and topics that are uncomfortable in some way and to hold space for those poets to tell their stories freely. My vision was for my editing of each book to be light, to help provide clarity to the poet's story, and to be in the form of suggestions, not demands made through my lens of seeing and experiencing the world.

The books in this series have been, and will continue to be, lightly touched by my hand so the poet's words shine through just as they intended. These books hold the author's stories, not mine, and as such, I have opened the gate for those words to flow uncensored and unredacted.

I read through a lot of manuscripts before selecting Anton Yakovlev's, and I selected his because the speaker's voice—a voice of haunting beauty, lyricism, and pain—stayed with me long after I finished. With time and thoughtful discussion, this manuscript became *One Night We Will No Longer Bear* the Ocean, and this title seems apt because reading this book is an act of bearing witness to the trauma of unrequited love—an act so close to home for many of us.

I chose this book as the second in the series, and to follow the inaugural book by the magical Maureen Seaton, because her book gave voice to another deep pain: the pain of dying and leaving this world. I see these two Redacted Series books as siblings in their trauma, grieving siblings who understand and speak to each in the language of shared pain—a pain so beautifully expressed in music.

Some may argue that music isn't poetry, and poetry isn't music, but it's much harder to argue that there isn't music in poetry. Maureen and Anton are both musicians in this sense to me: masters of rhythm, lyricism, and the beauty of words carefully arranged on the page for the joy of your ear. Listen closely as you read, speak the words aloud, and you too will hear the music come through.

Thank you so much for reading.

With love and gratitude,

Nicole Tallman
Miami, Florida
May 9, 2024

*So give me your hand as we part. That's better*
*than nothing. Our parting is solemn, lofty,*
*since it is forever. The zither's silent.*
*Forever is not a word, but a number,*
*whose unending zeroes, when grass grows above us,*
*will stretch out beyond our small time, our epoch.*

Joseph Brodsky, "Adieu, Mademoiselle Véronique"
Translated by George L. Kline

*Otherwise this stone would seem defaced*
*beneath the translucent cascade of the shoulders*
*and would not glisten like a wild beast's fur:*

*would not, from all the borders of itself,*
*burst like a star: for here there is no place*
*that does not see you. You must change your life.*

Rainer Maria Rilke, "Archaic Torso of Apollo"
Translated by Stephen Mitchell

# Table of Contents

# At the Airport Hotel

I kept passing my hand on the velvet comforter.

Nothing in the room had come from a grave.

It was dusk, and the statue of Edward Snowden
was working overtime to track the deletions
in my last email to you.

All those words I had refused.

They were all on the bed now, slowly
crawling off the edges,
stinging our bare feet.

And we sat on the corners
facing in opposite directions.

We could already hear the bulldozers.

I

# Everything Thrown Out          Except for Our Eyes

meeting across the river, not noticing the vomiting dog
         well, that's the architecture
of love: steeples of inattention, pits of catharsis, coffins of hurry
           these details mattered
to exactly zero mourning doves
        later, we also noticed each other's postures
the train was delayed, or just never scheduled
          so we took each other's hand
the endless pounding of the clock broken at midnight
        the operatic puppets grimaced wildly
dangerous books were getting burned in the most
           beautiful square
when the fire was done, one of the mandolinists forgot to leave
and was seen playing all through the night and into the next generation
the wind blew cinders into his nostrils
        censors made snow angels in the ashes
I bought you half a flower but got distracted
          a wasp pollinated it
next year there will be millions of half-flowers
        nocturnal birds will be hired to weed them

# Bedside Paperback

I entered the flower shop with tears in my eyes,
bought you flowers, and told you about my dead.
You cried vicariously then dove in a swimming pool
in search of a wedding ring you had lost years ago.
Frost was writing guitar chords on windows.

We went to the movies and watched a scatological fantasy.
We discovered things about each other
only the saddest sadists could tolerate.
Our respective families wrote poems and buried them
in shallow graves. A vulture circled our dogs
then flew away, knowing his time would come.

But sometimes a volcano surprises you, erupting in sunset colors.
We kissed in a dying town's town hall.
We did not run into any crucifixions on the way.
We built cabinets and read books together.
Our voices carried to the other side of the mountain.
Our smiles went viral. Birds were named in our honor.

And now neither of us knows what to do about
our unrequited love for each other.

# A Coloring Workbook on the Elements

Tell me how you're feeling, send in the little birds.
Send in the little birds, my sadness is not with them.
My sadness is not with them. It lives in a forest
of headless statues with golden hair, young diplomat.
Stop bouncing around, little bird, notice me slouching.

The boy that brought your favorite music to Europe
was eaten half by accident at a banquet.
Henry Ford often spent his weekends trafficking human lungs.
All human history smells like boots. Notice my face in the pavement.
Lighten the tips of your hair. I will follow them up.

As long as we both shall live, people will cut fruit.
People will cut fruit till they die. But you are still young.
Munch sinners, the preachers say, this is what you must do.
Don't let them cut your green eyes and harvest the broccoli.
Leave me a white trail, little airplane. That is all I could ever want.

The boy that brought you in on a ship from Europe
has forgotten the name on your passport.
Henry Ford thinks repentant thoughts as you fall diagonal off the bed.
The tips of your hair are blacker now, like the end of a candle lighter.
Just another night in Rhode Island. Then we can go.

# Anxiety

And all the cashiers in the chocolate store loved us.
No occasion to dream of poison. So much was said
through eye contact, even when there was none.
Our little corner welcomed blossoms while
we sat speed reading. No restraining orders.
Not that much death. The endorphins
of a harmless question holding onto
the face across the water. A walking tour
of an office park, a marina, a labyrinth, a novella—
everything rhymed. My family an indispensable cairn,
pines on the seashore. Silence at the movies.
Memory. It got colder. The cashiers smiled.
You sat for hours in the graveyard. I liked
holiday lights and peeking into embassies on Sunday.
We soaked our feet in puddles. Eyes closed, you painted.
And when we imagined spies all around, we touched.
No matter the play we went to, it was the way
our knees pressed against each other. One day you got a tattoo
but the waves washed it off. One moment no whales
were visible; the next moment no whales were visible.
Not that much death. We attended canonization
parties together. Hot-air balloons touched waterfalls.
Satellites flew too high to see or to hear.

# Your Voice

You make impressions without finishing touches

You fight philosophy with your homegrown Monadnock hymn

Your portable xylophones herd the pretentious beautiful

Your weapons aren't obvious

At length the oxygen starts running out and instead of enchantment with
   your consciously limited number of breaths per minute I start to yearn
   for the canyon outside, the one in which you can still find a stray
   guillotine here and there

If guillotines could sing, would they sing in your voice?

If I spoke in your voice, how quickly would I catch fire?

# Bedtime

I Zen my way through your legato tale
of balding Mensa men you've grown to hate.
I nod and clasp your hand but know I've failed
to grasp your zeitgeist. Plus it's getting late.
I challenge you to figure out how come
my late coworker's statues had me floored
far beyond *David*—but a sudden calm
has come upon you. Then a dainty snore.
What opiates did we take? A hand withdrawn?
Too many arguments over the phone
not jeweled with a make-up promenade?
Let's write a power ballad, scorn defeat,
ride centaurs, throw a steampunk masquerade!
You sleep. Half-open curtains smell of feet.

# Eventually the Scenery Changed

The path we followed
got covered in Middle-Earth moss, and we smiled,
but not at each other.

Just beyond the river, a rehearsal at the opera house
sounded like ricocheting bullet
points of our past arguments.

The moss turned into dirt then back into moss.
The landscape resembled a blown-apart sushi roll.
(Disrespectful) jokes boomeranged between us.

—

The idea of letting go of your dreams is really something *you* have to let go of.

But for now, you latch on to whatever is playing on your TV:

- A boxing match between two famous creationists
- The man who unfroze his wife for nothing

You cry, remembering an imagined version
of a recent disaster that did not go
at all
the way you had intended.

—

Talk to me. Tell me your symphonies.
There's so much in your demonology.
Including your fractal calm and those excellent,

excellent non-sequiturs. You furnish
sentences with unexpected chairs
for listeners to fall into. For example,

you start with the cellophane. Mr. Cellophane, that is.
He will always get well-paying gigs because he can be counted on to mooch.
Yeah, he's a politician.

Now Mr. Cellophane whips out a snowboard, and we're on Forget-Me
    Mountain.
Lots to think about on Forget-Me Mountain.
Like those funiculars that adjust themselves automatically based on who
    looks at them.
Doesn't mean they'll make themselves comfortable
                                        for you.

—

I don't anticipate your cars and your pillows. I don't anticipate
your cold war. I don't want your scholars playing the cello.
Your harmonica is lacking in color.
Your harmonica is lacking.

I see you with nothing around.
You could look at garbage and protest,
or you could begin somewhere else. You are traveling,
traveling. You are the forest. There is rain everywhere.

What am I on about? I'm glad it falls on you.

—

Here, here, talk to me a bit more.
Talk to me. Who are you? Who are you?
Have you ever been a long-distance runner?
Who do you latch on to now?
Where is your brain? Why is your brain a mashed potato? Do you know I
    love you no matter what?

You do not speak to me. You do not speak to me at all. I think of watermelons
    being run over by a combine.

I hang on to people no one else talks to.
I tell them our story. They tell me stuff
I already know, but now that I hear it from them,
everything is slightly off, as though
I'm looking at things with a taxidermy bird's eye.

I've got to do something about this uncontrollable urge
                                                      to save your life.

# The Line Between Our Lanes

Our rifts will grow into award-winning fog,
an army of God's little cows under our feet.

Tomorrow's most remarkable phenomenon
will be the titanium texture of honeysuckle.

You'll hide your hand in your sleeve
and wind God's gramophone.

I'll taste the three-orchestra oratory
we never got tickets for.

The grim reaper will grow a beard
right out of his skull.

Someone will take notes.

# Previously Owned by God

there are cauldrons of hot wax in our basement
we've been making Monty Python of our gradual drifting apart
we watch playground basketball not wanting to face each other
we'll never get over the exit signs over the exits we took together

someone I know doesn't walk through the open door
and there it stands and I write a small dissertation
there are rabbits who will kill half of our armies with a single tooth
there are cows previously owned by God now living in our bedroom

we make the basketballs deflate with our eyes
I won't be able to go to our mutual friend's funeral
you say I'm shooting with a sparrow at a philosophy
and I'm the only one who understands your inflection

sometimes the music between us is safer than a black hole
sometimes we have no weapons at all

# Your Windmills Can Set Down Their Fireworks

You're losing me in counterfeit Tarot cards,
in lines you've written hoping for someone else
to slow your fall through the Earth. I write
incomprehensible lyrics to be alone with your God.

Don't look for me. I'm hanging out in your lobby,
but you left months ago. You were born and died
almost immediately according to that bystander.
Memories crash into my frozen yogurt.

You're losing me when you say you're a spirit world.
You're losing me when you say you're death.
I do not look for you in the early bird parking lots.
I do not look for you in the grapefruit shrubs.

I wanted to keep you alive;
now I'm an iPad streaming
news that never took place. I'm missing
the most important part of your parade.

I should be arrested for having lingered
this long. You ring like a carnival, and
no one understands you're a manuscript
left in someone else's Saragossa.

I see you in a forgotten coliseum.
I see you now as I never saw you
in 1200 BC. I'm so scared I only
spoke to the God in you.

# Timor Mortis Conturbat Me

I took my time compartmentalizing with exotic relish
but eventually did shipwreck into your apartment's
cracked-asphalt blue mountain, just in time for my haze
to hike in again. I couldn't get enough
of your unsentimental photo abyss
which could also be used as a folding ghost
of dominant watersheds. I cleaned clocks,
keeping tranquility above legends.

Falling asleep to our elegiac Augustan fuckups
was salubrious enough, but our purple ground
me to cricket flour. Rogers and Hammerstein
pedaling is such an elusive science.

My faith in humanity was good and gone by the time
your fireproof circular token cult clashed with
the battalions in me—something you didn't spot
until too late. Chopin jazzed the three blind mice.
If only you had known more preemptively
what I meant. Soon nothing more existed.

# Frog Pond

Your parade of suicidal catamarans
cut such an enticing shooting-star
curve in my oubliettes,
I told you I enjoyed spending time with you
in a clearance summer
in a vacuum timetable.

I didn't do a lot of breathing.

But no matter how much you sang,
your teeth were Stonehenge,
or typewriter keys.

My pastor told me your commuter rail
was made of wooden beetles,
so I made myself sleepy.

I was a kettle
and you an ice cream accident.

Tonight, in a throwback compound,
your flag has shadowed the grass
I'm made of.
You look at me.

Sorry, homey.

Your ghost has solidified.

# Coffins of the Living

*You see them everywhere once you've trained your eye: in the photos of birch buds interrupted by bird heart attacks, in the Salvation Army's medusa gaze, in the executioners' staycations, in the overheating grandfather pendulums.*

You stopped your grandfather clock so it wouldn't disturb me. I stayed awake all night waiting for its next ring. By morning, you were wearing a scarf of sleeping flies.

*Avenue of the Americas gets me every time. Here I am, walking with my peanut butter milkshake, late rain dripping off all those statues with misspelled names—and here they come, the coffins: twisted like researchers, sudden like urban redwoods.*

Toward the end, your house had almost no furniture. A bit like you— beautifully Victorian, but nothing really there anymore. When you gave me a hug, your door pounded the back of my head.

*In my dream, I saw beautiful coffins. They were coughing, sneezing, spewing random insults and pink mist through their unfinished hinges. Some would have pictured them as priests. Others would have hidden in them.*

You started to walk on the wrong side of the trampoline. You started your sentences at their deaths. Every time I checked in on you, you looked like you had mutated into a jazz song. At times, they opened bridges in Amsterdam.

*April began with a couple of startlingly disarming guitar chords before becoming a coffin itself. My brain was mostly on the outside of my skull by then.*

You lived through anonymous yard sale ticks, immigrant political detachments, and shotgun goodwill. You pointed the muzzle of your omnipotence at all the wrong tuxedos. I turned my head the wrong way. I was afraid of still seeing you as the Sun.

*The most honest of us sleep in our coffins.*

I still look at that photo you took of me, wearing film strips under the heat lamp.

II

# The Car You Drove That Night Was Silver

I used to dialogue with your poplar blossoms.
Swinging in hammocks,
I shared with you my whatever.
You set the tone for my snapshots
of seagulls, of faith,
lent tastefulness to my grab bags.
You were easy to talk to,
easy to hug in ballrooms.
Your notes fell into my day like weather.

—

A man came in from the cold.
It was *very* cold. It was coonskin cap time
for him. He headbanged that striped tail,
a pioneer. He was awkward.
He flaunted an irresistible wavelength.
Later, you walked the streets shivering.
You got support from friends who orbited you.
You learned to make cupcakes
and followed cats across bridges.

—

I wonder why I can no longer hum
any of your carols. From swings,
I can tell you nothing.
Your curls are somewhere.
I wouldn't be able to tell what apple horseradish
you mix and match. I wouldn't be able to tell
your lips from cough drops. I don't know your coat-of-arms.
I wonder if cloud nine rained at any point.
I wonder if that water saved any trees.

# The Cedar Creek

We steep tea and then we read about tea and then we steep it some more and then we read some more and there is just so much we need to say to each other. The moment you tell me the truth I fall in the cedar creek. It's not my fault, nor is it yours, but now our neighborhood is not the same. We do not taste chocolate the same way. Can I forgive you? No, not really. Not at all. Go fall into a volcano. I'll be the volcano. I'll pick you up after the show trial.

I would have liked to linger on your face. I used to wait for you by the cedar creek. After all, plenty of scholars keep their careers alive with thoughts of you. You juggle torches even when people kiss you. I would have liked to nestle with your world, but a world can destroy a rowboat. A lifelong addict, you are now clean and a spy, but you ripple like a head-scratcher. The cedar creek keeps adjusting its watershed.

You no longer balk at decomposition. You compose a symphony to be played with metal hooks on dead things. You stand in front of the cedar creek and don't reveal any secrets. You resort to Russian anti-Napoleonic strategies, which is to say you bravely choose to let Moscow burn. A general is wise to let the other general self-destruct.

I do. The leitmotifs come back. We argue and we clutch. We go to Jesus Christ and bite into the infinite bread. Will we ever move beyond our lack of cue balls? The cedar creek never did turn into wine. Your fear touches me like a bouncing night.

# Catching Up

The man who is dead to me
stands next to me
in a crowded ballroom.
We make polite conversation.

Safely stowed away inside his hat,
the things he's done
almost don't show.

No one else speaks to him,
too intimidated by his genius.

Someone works up the nerve to offer him a cigar.
His fingers slink
like eels.

He puffs at the cigar, and circles of
betrayals envelop the ballroom.

This man used to be my friend.

He wants to go off and mingle
and asks me to leave without a goodbye.
(I destroy a napkin.)

A spotlight follows him
around the room.

# Betrayal

The moment midnight rings, you throw on your coat
and wear your hat at a deliberate angle.
It forms a solid unit with your face
and turns you into a Raphaelite portrait.

Out in the real world, skulls rise out of the snow.
Femurs and phalanges crack underfoot.
Maggots make waves in newly-thawed puddles.
Disconnected jaws hop across the street.

For half a block, we walk alongside each other.
I can almost hear the gears in your head:
"I have so many answers for you," you think.

A maggot lands between your eyes,
your award-winning eyes.

You run a willow branch along your cheek.
Buds fall off one by one.

# A Table for Two Scrapes the Floor

Sitting in my apartment
        to discuss an estranged friend's tragedy,
you sip so much Merlot you forget the reason you called.

The hats your family wears are a tragedy in themselves.

You talk to me for hours about baby sadness,
        about all the prank obituaries you write.

I love your voice. I'm thinking:
Hold antique dolls against your fashionable dress.
Knock me off my chair,
           shaking paprika off the table.

—


        Then you say:
Let us search together for absent friends.
    I say yes but whisper:
I have nothing to do with you.

When you leave, I look for the passing shadows
of a beowulf,
        still visible across dimming hills,
pulling me into the streets.

        I only see your car
departing past the cracking fireworks.
        I only see dead squirrels
neatly packed against the edge of the sidewalk.

—

I sleep on manholes,
            listening to the trains underneath.

Tomorrow I will be chasing everything.
I will sit alone at our table,
                    waiting for it to shake.

# Wildlife

you've given up drinking so
you politely refuse it
you leave your purse behind
and let momentum take you
past the Potemkin
until you stop on the bridge
and if some stranger asks you
whether the man you love is alive
the green domes
promise a full ride
and a wedding
you're relieved at the cold rain
from your pocket
colors have gone all sunset
the tree house from which your feet dangled
now only a miracle

if someone hands you a glass
you spill it in their face
at The Tower Room
across Vasilevskiy
graffiti building façade
outside the Sports subway station
you won't be clear
or dead
of Annunciation Temple
fellowship to the sky
at a chapel in heaven
you take out a photo
yourself as a little girl
corners pure fingerprint
pure wildlife
can reverse your Laika flight

# The Minimalist Muzak

I take the elevator down into a drawing of my own life.
The minimalist muzak creaks like a shallow grave.
Back when you liked the colors of my shirts,
I liked being parked on the side of the highway with you.

Now all my shirts are ugly, so I drive you to your apartment.
Our talk is small. We won't discuss the time
our tortures sounded similar enough to church bells
for us to get married. Let sleeping dogs shut up.

The garden is a beating heart, but so is the desert, and I
was the nobody you wrote about. You take the elevator
up to your grave apartment while I linger in the mud
eating the offspring of your birthday cakes.

It's not your birthday, and I don't want to remember you,
but somehow you woke up the entire animal shelter.
Someone said you were moving up in the world.
The muzak was so strange you forgot to be angry.

We tried to visit every friendly face on the island,
but our third meaning must have gotten overexposed.
Everything is clearer with the highway empty.
Everything was parked by our side. Where did it go?

# After

We board the ferry with nothing further to hide

A passing truck means everything to someone

The ferryman of death stands by in his coma

Albatrosses hang everywhere

We spoke through tremors

You ate from the sky's dead hands

Now fortunes hang in lanterns

Humans walk around without language

I fall asleep on the headstone of your hypocrisy

# God Under Your Bare Feet

What did you know? The Moon snapped photos till
substitute Moons arrived. Ghosts and trash blew
across the park. After five years you said
the word for the first time—that isn't what
brought me to you. We were used to being
weeds; now we wait like statues at the crosswalk.
The red hand won't turn. Wish you had clipped
my song in your Gordian hair. You looked
at me before we melted. Silence of
your shirt. We rode the green wave. The gas station
became a church. It will be years until
the dead are added up. Rain whips the bears
in the dark. I remember the exit ramp,
the radio, lanes blending into sleep,
the question in the rearview mirror.

# I Held You Like a Pencil Drawing

That was my first mistake.
Whoever expected us to become the best movie of the decade
needs to go home and become a better person.
The rain stayed right where it fell.
Even shadows failed better than we. Perhaps
I could have still become your John the Baptist.
You wouldn't have had to be Salome.
Funny how a hand gesture can make one's year. One second
you're a statue in a crypt; the next second you're a full Moon.
Tides of skyscrapers obeyed you. Birds learned your songs.
Dogs bit each other at not having you in their lives.
I could have jumped in the rip tide, but a park ranger
stopped me. I think about your lost photo albums,
what iceberg has now absorbed them in the Arctic Ocean.
Who doesn't know the feeling? You dive—and there it is,
nibbled by belugas. And then you take up residence
in the neighboring coast guard station and drink.
Who wouldn't? For six months you stare at a sketch
of an aborted pipeline. Eventually it gets easier.
You go back to your ancestral secondary city.
A skeleton of a boy you knew rules the landscape.

# You Were a Traffic Jam

that rushed forward just to see
if the wind you create could open some windows.
You were thrown by how many windows you opened and
turned back into a parking lot.
    I threw open a window after some yoga.
    It stung me to see
    cars grind to a halt
    as soon as I showed.


You were a performer biting your nails onstage
until they gave you a javelin.
With the words "not to be"
you hurled it into the audience.
    I was teaching myself to perform random acts of evil.
    I never attended your play but pretended I had,
    came to offer congratulations and couldn't see
    why my hug caused you to break down.


You were a parking meter that got fed up
with people's money and decided to give free time
but balked at the cars
now smashing each other to reach you.
    I landed squarely in your parking spot.
    I tell you, the last thing I expected to see
    was a pancake of melted metal
    where the parking meter once stood.


You were an immigrant snake
that came all the way across
the Atlantic by burrowing underground
but got careless once you got on dry land.

I was a turkey suffering from remorse
over having pecked a kitten to death.
When my comrades started to peck you,
I tried to save you from them. I swear I did.

You were a boat notorious for its grit.
People always tried to put holes in you
and failed, until you took pity on their sad toes
and quietly sank yourself when no one was watching.
    I wasn't up to any funny business,
    just came to the marina to scrape barnacles,
    only to discover a drowned human
    who had floated out of a sunk boat.

You were a library obsessed
with being ahead of its time.
As soon as you heard of e-books,
you got rid of all the paper inside you.
    I was an architect that came to the site
    of the razed library, tasked with filling the spot
    with something decent. I thought about it a bit
    and built another library in your place.

You were a second-hand cupcake tray
that disappeared among the pots and the pans
of a neighborhood store,
never to be heard from again.
    I would have bought you right then.
    Really, I would have.
    In fact, I really had a sweet tooth.
    But I was a horseman of the Apocalypse.

# Chicken

Like
     any other day, the country was troubled,
flapping
        its upside-down flags from the shotgun poles.
We needed
         to test how much we meant to each other
and drove each
        other off the cliff. The corpse
we landed on didn't
         smell yet, which was bizarre,
as it had lain there for
        at least two hundred
years, and even longer
        according to some.
Windshield wipers waved
         relentlessly,
and beauty never came to the
        rescue.

Years later, the dog keeps whistling.

Who won?
        Unrequited rhetorical
questions provide their own orgasm.

# The Self-Conscious Gorgeousness of Sunsets

When the only person who understood you wishes you dead,
the smell of an approaching forest fire feels like a footnote.
Your best friend's best friend the only victim.
The fire stopped at your house.

Each morning the dogs found skeletons of burnt songbirds.
Each morning you looked at the vodka bottle under your window.
Your father's wrinkles so much more pronounced now.
The Moon was never made more orange by fires,

but imagining so gave you comfort. You tried to break
every chair you sat on, always failed, and dreamed
of setting them aflame with your Yankee candle.
Your friends insisted on driving you everywhere.

When you chewed gum, they made homicidal faces.
Paintings bled off walls. In the self-conscious
gorgeousness of sunsets religions threatened to form.
Burnt clay pigeons survived for five thousand years.

III

# Never Come to Terms

Do I start with the Ionian village? Call it fairweather? Mention a woman who
turns a local chicken incantatory, aping it with gestures and voice?

Do I admit that my mind keeps going to the possible whales out of sight?
Do I admit that I wonder about their bathroom habits and deaths?

I submerge myself in upside-down rain
and make like a dying whale, enter spoiled-egg world.

To tell the truth, people laugh at my model trains, but they are
merely unrecognizable covers of songs none of you remember.

Why should I unmake myself? Even the most
comfortable cats will envy my future,

plough through the seasons, pieces of birds in their mouths,
and never come to terms. Who am I kidding?

The wings (even the cat) flap, resonate with the cozy
epiphany. Say what you will: it's there.

It shoves its plankton at you while you're underwater
till you're all green and nostrils flare with news.

You've learned nothing. Who cares?
As ever, you're ready to tread the shattering water.

# Break

Sunlight looks great on your brush
but no paint ever sticks to the canvas
and how can you burn a painting until there *is* a painting?
Throw your paint and see it stop in mid-air.

Air rolls in air, polluted with Prince Oblonsky smiles.

They rolled away your baby grand years ago,
and did you ever believe in hammers?

You could write a letter to a lapsed friend, detailing
that restless cardinal's rap chorus outside
your window. You know that could be enough.

Something squats in your aorta.

Lately you've been overcomplicating things
like love, drowning it in folklore.

Booze feels like ballroom dancing.

Your doppelgänger is a pizza joint
in the township on the other side of the median
covered with cartoons
full of ambition
to make miracles you can't get rid of.

Visitors write religions on paper planes.

Death would validate things, but its microphone is broken.
Better wait for another god to roll by.

After all, it's twenty minutes to your next brain.

# The Forgotten Years

Slammed a wall in halo creation process
Packed a holy twister into a postcard
Rags are lifted from cooling corpses
Hoping for a chance encounter, but the churches

Packed a holy twister into a postcard
On a night of rarely worn sunglasses
Hoping for a chance encounter, but the churches
Converge to view a punctuated flashback

On a night of rarely worn sunglasses
Human bodies expand, some twelve hours later
Converge to view a punctuated flashback
Unambiguously marked on a wooden pole

Human bodies expand, some twelve hours later
Faces become mountains through the window
Unambiguously marked on a wooden pole
In your garden that turned to silence

Faces become mountains through the window
Fallen out of syntax, music lost color
In your garden that turned to silence
Hummingbirds illuminated. Repeated breathing

Fallen out of syntax, music lost color
Slammed a wall in halo creation process
Hummingbirds illuminated. Repeated breathing
Rags are lifted from cooling corpses

# The Diaries in the Flats Have Biodegraded

Few people know about the right-of-way that explains
the weedy strip of land stretching from town to town.
The railway agency has owned it for a century,
postponing and postponing railroad construction.

Imaginary commuters hop on and off in a sweat.
Imaginary suicides hang out in the nettles.
Nonexistent trains make division-by-zero noise,
inhibiting every attempt to reuptake meditation.

Another winter, and I'm still alone on my porch,
watching the drawbridge that rarely opens.
I see myself as the last circulating copy
of a panned film I never bothered to see.

Some afternoons, experimental music arrives
from acquaintances who once refused to be my
friends but still want my opinion. Were I on a journey
of self-creation, I would have blown up the speakers.

If I had children, they would have told me to stay
exactly where I am for the rest of my life.
Everyone is better for it, I sigh, spooking
the mountain lion that only drops by in my mind.

# Memoir

I hoped it would be trickier than that.
But I could never catch that wrecking ball.
Beer on the porch. A purifying cat.
I hoped it would be trickier than that.
Cremated to a crisp, the urn all set,
no bones to grind, no children to console—
I hoped it would be trickier than that.
But I could never catch that wrecking ball.

# The Grass Highway

When people come to the city, they try to choose
apartments closest to it, to feel its greenery.
The marshland air circulating within its pores
protrudes through tires and often ends up in dreams.
Made from the same grass as the tennis courts,
one of the more unusual nineteenth-century
landmarks of Cambridge, the Grass Highway can take you
all the way to the old bathhouses if you let it,
or it can let you cloud-watch, ecstatically undisturbed,
on the quiet evenings when the Sun plunges,
hovercraft-like, into every neighborhood attic.

Before the automobile was invented
horses used to march on it just as beautifully,
riders gaining brief solace from life's bureaucracy,
knowing they will be late but still taking the long road
to feel the grass, pneumatic under their hooves.
Then, like a maverick rabbit mating in the off-season,
Lumières' invention populated the theater
in Medford, and the highway became a rite
of passage for dressed-up couples inside their beeping Volkswagens,
every Friday, on their way to forgetting
their terminal illness, for a minute, coffee in hand,
to the piano sounds of a silent film.

During the war it fell into disrepair.
Bullfighters used the highway to drag dead bulls
to the slaughterhouses in North Cambridge.
No one else was around, everyone was gone.
Dying on French soil for people they didn't know,
they couldn't have cared less for the bulls that were killed.

Absorbing the blood of a different bull each day,
the highway drastically changed its character.
Many a car disappeared on it in the evening;
the neighborhood became a hotbed of voodoo.
And so, in the early 1950's, the highway closed
along with all the twelve corridas of Cambridge.

—

An overachieving bullfighter with no other marketable skills,
for twenty years I wandered the highway,
unable to get a job even at a rendering plant,
where rotting bulls get processed in the same tank
with puppies. I was little more than a ghost at sunset,
crowning the highway with my silhouette.
For twenty years I was its only landmark.
But then people wondered what that empty field was about.
They looked at paintings of the highway's past,
liked what they saw, raised money, purchased machinery—
and so, after decades of weeds and forgetting,
the highway reopened in 1972.

Stuck in the middle of the highway for ten thousand years
in my own personal purgatory, after some careless fellow
killed me with his car soon after the reopening,
I window-watch the ladies on the highway each morning,
driving to their jobs at electrical corporations,
with their revealing dresses and gothic hair,
to do accounting. Once again they are late,
once again they smell the smell of skunks
and do not mind it, once again the reflection
of their car's metal in the grass turns their heads.
Looking at the pink flowers upon their dresses,

I fondly recall my victories over bulls,
the blood and the roses after.

These days, people mostly kill bulls online,
pointing their high-bandwidth, low-resolution
cameras at them, plunging remote-controlled
spikes into them, all the while drinking beer
in front of their computer in their underwear,
email and pornography open in other windows.
Anyone can be a matador these days.
They never even see the bulls they have killed,
whom servicemen feed to dogs or donate to shelters
of dogs, or dispatch straight to rendering plants.
Strangers buy protein drinks with bits of their tendons,
unaware of the ground-up animals' online history
or the blood across the asphalt highways of Spain.

In Spain, just like here, there are lots of ghosts on the highways
and naked people in attics, shooting distant animals
over the internet, for rangers to overnight them
in parts, or pass on their antlers to maritime hook-up clubs
where middle-aged couples snort them in place of cocaine,
nostalgic for their love in the days of disco.
I was already a ghost in the days of disco,
a ghost throwing long gazes across the Grass Highway,
thinking melodious thoughts when Cadillacs passed me
on Friday nights; still thinking when the same clubs
closed for off-season renovations; still thinking
when they went out of style and were shredded by bullets.
Locked up in infinite silence, I drew lines on the grass.

—

When you take a ride on the highway this Thursday
with your longtime sweetheart and a bouquet of roses,
take care to notice the traffic divider lines,
the way you have to turn your car upside down
twelve times as the highway curves around downtown Cambridge.
Take care to notice the blood, still visible in the grass,
of all the bulls that succumbed to my iron, close-combat spikes
before I would myself succumb to a car
much like your own, with tires made up of sweet dreams.
That night you will go back to your lover bereft of energy,
hardly able to speak, and only after a nap
on top of both of the pillows you once gave each other
will you finally reveal all the ugly reasons you love her.

And the leprosy from which you barely recovered
last summer will manifest itself in the roses she has sewn into
her dress, as you see their thorns draw blood from her body
when she whispers, "Someday you too will commit suicide."
The breakup will go on long past midnight,
with past admissions of love erased by apology,
with countless pieces of memory chipping off
and falling across the traffic divider lines
until you scream and pass out, and dream the dreams of the horses
walking the highway centuries ago,
when it was only a field, and people needed strange shoes
to walk across to the other part of the city
and not succumb to the cryptic stuff of old legends.

And every now and then those who could not afford
shoes would get lost in the field and turn into bones,
and folk tales would be composed by the hovering warblers
witnessing the faces of their dead skulls.
You will talk to the grandchildren you'll never have,

and you will sleep, convinced that your heart has burst
sometime at night, drawing a curtain on you;
and you will not care, and even find certain peace;
and you will live with this feeling for many minutes
until you hear the dirty noise of the sun
coming back from under your cellar of rotting apples
and, hearing the measured chugging of the rendering plants,
understand that a new day has arrived.

# I've Sat on This Perch for Decades, and Now It's Time to Get Up

I told them it wasn't me bending into the world.
They were too busy rolling their eyes to hear.
They were a demolished movie theater
gone slightly radioactive. All the park benches were empty,
and all the roadkill had been cleared away.

We ignore the dim bespectacled eyes. One day,
the departed play poker on their own monuments:
A haircut that looked like a pie. A scholar who stood
on his head. The eagle burrows into the center
of the Earth and gets stuck there, victim of gravity.

But even after the militants destroy the statue
tears of blood appear every morning under
the empty pedestal. The poets with varicose veins
pirouette around the fire. The fall foliage is so seductive
in the glow. Dogs tap dance. Rearview mirrors reflect no past.

Lighthouses broadcast koans. More flash photography.
Temporary anathema. Mountains in the shapes
of missed handshakes. All the rotten bodies. Take your
boredom, sculpt a soulmate. You don't know what's hiding
along the theatrical highway you drove all night.

# How to Keep Warm

Leave your home. Turn left onto Ungrip Street,
drive down the hill past the statues
with erased names. The mine is a mound now,
no strikers and no canaries. Lie down on it.

Put your side to the softest moss.
The fires have burned underground since the 1960s.
Ignore the combine coming toward you.
Squint at the Sun rising between the farms.

When your eyelids can feel again, drive back to Magone
where your friend's godlike nephew sells grape pies.
Ask him to microwave one. Don't gulp the coffee.
Take a walk. Never mind the Field of Bad Weather.
It's not as bad as the river you're swimming across.

Try out the bison knocker on the mayor's door.
Remember when she showed up to your sci-fi reading?
Tell her what's on your amygdala. Don't worry about the clichés.
Don't think of all the bands that broke up after hearing your story.
Take heart that someone is still spilling blood for you.

They bury moose just beyond the edge of Down County.
Over time their skeletons slide into what used to be the river.
Bury your feet in that future pool of petroleum.
Your warmest memory will land on you like a hat.

Run down Fist Closed Road, clutching the residual heat.
At noon, the train carrying your heart to a safe
destination will trundle along Manic & Pacific.
Work up a sweat as you run up to its green windows,
unclench your fist, and trace a flame in the frost.

# I Hope You're Wonderful

These days, if I make my bed, I see your heart
untucking itself from my pillow and falling out
onto the defunct horse farm I only pretended to own

when you were around. Our respective continents
drift past each other in a planet of blood. You were
too beautiful to wear anything, and so you took off

my sunglasses. Now I live in the blinding weather
your eyes were two years ago. Would that they were a cloud.
Would that you were a self-conscious clown,

a slumped ambassador from the reticent side of the wall.
I wave at you with an irresponsible grin. Your hologram
waves back at me from a New England cranberry bog,

the only place where things made sense to you for a time.
On the world's worst mountain, they still remember
the quickness of your eyes scanning the graves

of the almost-successful climbers. A mere outline of a man
climbed alongside you, lighter than a day off.
Later, when you whispered despair to me in the car,

love fell out of my ear into our shared coffee.
You climbed your ladder high enough
to see us both in the coffin.

None of this really matters.
Your shadows sprinkle the desert.
I never asked you the questions you were convinced

I swatted you with, never fitted my truck with trinkets of you.
Revisiting all the places we had tucked each other in,
I keep my hazard lights on. You wouldn't want to

talk to me, anyway. I don't care to meet
the horrid bird you plan to become this year.
I never thought of our intertwined fingers

as a ladder to anything other than ourselves.

# Adorable

I look at the raccoons from far away
remembering the minutes when you cared.
The rocks, the daylight, the buttermilk bay.
I look at the raccoons from far away.
Their rabies would have troubled you today.
You were so close; now you've disappeared.
I look at the raccoons from far away
remembering the minutes when you cared.

# I Throw Boulders Out of My Window Sometimes

Your memory, a whimsical stump, still fools me.

Screeching thump-dreams wake me up in the morning,
creep like plants along the walls of the house.

I go to the pinball machine—
your memory is right there, in the flowerpot.
I turn to the wall.

The ducks are silent.

Sometimes I see patterns of light on the radiator.

# Sometimes Your Name Appears on Random Paintings

The city drips like honey onto maps.
The quiet whoosh is different from dying.
Wings rain on us like yellow silhouettes,
silhouettes of time against the wall.
I tried to build a buffer from your bones
but knew you'd never understand. Truth is
a picture: naked, moderately guilty.
God pollinates the flowers the bees forgot.

# Marconi Seashore

Then, shooting those painterly marshes,
                    I saw you:
a nude silhouette reflected
                    in tidal pools,
sunset in every direction.
                    Of course, the salt
transmitted your soft voice
                    across the ocean.
The fishermen paid no mind to the similarity
                    between the dying fish
and your starring role in *The Rite of Spring*.
            I knew very soon
I'd feel you in the melting of my bones

when,
            waking up somewhere
on a tree-brushed train, your body,

still warm,
            catches up to kindness
knocking at your skull from the inside.

Chalk it up to
                    breathing, chalk it up to
the sweat of past mistakes
                    that soaks the grass, drowning
the wrong years.

                    The shutter clicked and clicked.

IV

# Key West

Awakened by a call from a human

I thought was dead

A city measured in panic

Flowers wilted so rapidly they made wind

I swam past sunrise off the Southernmost Point

All along the jetty until invisible

An anthem admitting all

A boy in the road full of models and advanced riddles

A dog dragging a chicken across and everyone clapping

Benches mostly of dust

I understood

# Exhibition Match

And so, after all that cheeky volcano stuffing,
after all those wannabe Bastille manifestos,
we finally find our shared history in a place
that yields itself to sequels, alternate versions,
authorized counterfeits and common misappropriations.
Our point of no return's jazzed-up cover songs
have made their way as far as some luxury diners'
hush-hush specials. Second-tier politicians
have taken to hawking pipelines connecting our shared sky
to assisted rumors of Martian fun.
                                        That said, I still can't
confidently predict what will happen to you in any given
three days, if you will keep your ordinary abyss
or take up residence in a church steeple. Because of that,
my hands don't work when I see you, or else I give hugs to fountains
instead of you. I half-remember our days of direct eye contact
the way a violin hallucinates. So, like any draft dodger,
I make cheat sheets to get me through the next time your lost vocal line
resurfaces in a wise-guy baseball opera.

Right now, for instance, you're nowhere. Your Cheshire scowl
still hovers above the street, and rumor has it not all your wallflowers
have wilted; but your bowling alley stands without juice
and all your abstracts are wrapped up in herring. My heart
skips a beat or six every time a racket flies through the air
in hopes your tennis muse has come flooding back.
Someone told me last night they saw you in Texas
on a tree-lined street where whispering is illegal.

Random subdivisions of public oxygen
get on my nerves more than ever.

Cyclops may be restless in their academic research,
but I smell nothing when I should smell continents,
and I look for your fingerprints in diners.
The lava flows. I count steps. A pre-failed neighbor walks
his dog with a Gregorian grimace.

To tell the truth, I'm quite tired. I used to want to write scriptures,
but now I call it a day at the music of tidal waves.
I guess that's why my low point, the one catharsis I allowed myself
over our demolished set design,
has been anthologized as lazing around
in front of you, a bliss just a ford too far,
too easy even for relics.

# At the James Joyce House

This is what I wanted to let you know:
when I came home last night, I found my building repainted:
property management had renamed it
from Ocean Plaza Apartments to James Joyce House,
probably trying to boost the rentals next year.

Neon lights above the front door displayed the new name
in genuine Joyce handwriting,
and all the condos had been rearranged
the way James Joyce would have done it.

The desk from which I had recited to you
our surrealism was replaced
with something faux Victorian.
The dining chairs were also Joycean:
an introductory booklet I found on the dinner table
made a big deal of the way they were stylized
so closely to his living room
you'd think he'd sat on every last one of them.

In the bathroom, the shells we had picked up
waddling for years around Cape Cod
were replaced with a single crumbling clam shell—
but that shell bore a genuine autograph of James Joyce.
The booklet boasted that property management
had handed me an antique worth twenty thousand dollars
just to pay me back for the inconvenience
of rearranging my rooms and throwing out half my things.

Honored as I am, this morning I spent two hours
looking for a rusty nail to dip into my Jameson—
the rustier the better.

I have no TV to distract me—
James Joyce didn't have one. So now neither do I.

The memory foam mattress on which we had lost
our virginities had been taken away,
now in a landfill. Not that I mind, of course.

And yet tears come out of my eyes for some reason
and I take walks to inspect the building's dead ends
looking for spots intact from remodeling,
trying to get back to a past that included you.

If you were here, though, the autograph of James Joyce
would have made it all worth it: you would have wept
on my shoulder to be so close to your hero.

I would have tried to talk to you about us,
but you would have circled back to "The Dead,"
to Leopold Bloom's unsavory diet,
to the goat-like creatures Stephen Dedalus had dreamed up.

A panther would have shrieked outside the window just then,
as we kissed, and you would have turned
your eyes to look at it,
acting like I wasn't even present.

That's okay, I'd say to myself.
At least you are here.

# For Here There Is No Place

I've cracked the vanity of geoengineering
and the need to live in caves for five hundred years.
I've predicted private nuclear weapons,
deciphered symbols of bigotry on some trump cards.
I've crashed cookouts with revolutionaries
on the wrong end of a burning national park.
But when they Skype me up,
flashing their press credentials,
all they want to know about
is my seven-year relationship.

I've filmed rollercoasters under the boots of soldiers.
I've fed dumbstruck children tales of exploding blimps,
only finding rest for an hour or two
in the triangular living room of an angry oat farmer.
I've noticed it usually rains on the nights I speak.
But when they ask about the source of my depression,
they fail to notice all the dead trees in the forest
and the garbage patches around the oceans.
They just want to know my ex's rating
on the attractiveness scale.

When I scoff at them, they liken me to a deer
stupidly dashing away from a Lego car.
They photograph my belly from below.
They wait till I open my mouth at a crooked angle
then invite an award-winning sketch artist to meld my face
onto the body of a beached whale.
I get into indie films, but they put a pomelo
in my mouth and laugh at my eyebrows.
They pay for an ad on the side of a passing train

condemning my manifesto on acid rain.
When I tell them to fuck off, they revoke my voice.

At a cafe, I'm one hundred seventy pages
into the second draft of my hardball reboot
of personal responsibility
when a honcho with an insecure grin
streams my ugly forehead to the world.
When I can't help but talk for several hours
to a disgraced firebrand with a stunning face,
a ripped lilac dress, and seventeen Twitter followers,
the honcho writes an editorial arguing
that I'm one of the world's bigger problems.

And so I dream of walking into the sea,
just melting into the waves. I want to
no longer care about the people who disown
family members for simply knowing my name.
I come back to the national park to see
if the revolutionaries are OK. I become
the firebrand's eighteenth follower and can't stop
tweeting at her until she agrees to meet me
for macchiato. I iron my best flannel shirt.

But the firebrand has googled me
and won't act normal until I tell her
all about my depression. Sure, she'll discuss
her documentary lit entirely by rockets,
but she always circles back to that seven-year relationship
that landed me in the hospital. And I'd resist her,
but there's something about her eyes.

And so I tell her of my ex's blush and curls,
and the cabbage kitchen we ran together,
and the charity she had made me a mascot of,
and my favorite goldfinches and philosophers,
and my symbolism-for-two, and my foggy mountain,
and our fights, and the hours I passed in my car
getting up the nerve just to see her again,
and our badminton of humiliation,
and my guilt the night I stopped feeling
anything, and her face on the day she told me
I objectively deserved to die.

The firebrand's blue hat rests on the coffee table and smiles
at us like a misplaced archaic
torso of Apollo. Nothing moves,
not even the doorframe. And the firebrand shrugs and must go.
And I waddle down my childhood avenue
in the general direction of my favorite stump in the forest,
the one on which I sat for hours one day
talking to my ex about zombies.

# Inverness

Before we know it, her car will screech down the hill
past cows with spots that look like music notation

on her way to a stage kiss. She tells me about
her hardest knock on the head, her corsets, her nightly

tumbles down ladders. We compare the colors
of our wheelbarrows, rummage through

our backpacks for signs of care.
Einstein said gaps between

bodies were an optical illusion.
"Through Eden took their solitary way"

assumes "in the same direction," how else did Adam and Eve
fall asleep that night and every other

night? Far below, serial riptides hurl their foam at the cliffs
as we walk away from each other.

# Derangement

Midway through the postproduction of a movie based on your life
I moved across the street from your apartment.

I shrunk from the thought that you might find out
I was making a movie based on your life.
So I ignored you, old friend, every time I passed you
in the street, pretending to be intense,
preoccupied with something oh-so-important.

But one winter afternoon I needed your advice
about getting involved with a charity you knew.
I called you up, as nonchalantly as possible,
forcing myself, in a moment of hard-earned self-control,
to ignore the fact that I was making a movie based on your life.

You offered your piece of mind happily, ramblingly.
However, your advice was so incredibly wrong
and revealed so many misguided assumptions
about the very fabric of human life,
I couldn't help wanting to correct you.

It was awkward, though: how dare I correct you
when I'm the one asking for help?
I rambled and rambled and rambled,
trying and failing and failing
to get to the point.

Suddenly I noticed that, during our conversation,
I had forgotten all about the movie based on your life
and didn't feel the least bit uncomfortable about it.

I patted myself on the back for that feat. Just then
you interrupted: "I really have to go, okay?"

I hurled my phone at the wall, gasping
as though you had torpedoed my solar plexus.
You were avoiding me!
You obviously hated me
for the movie I was making, based on your life!

For weeks after that, I only got more depressed
anytime I saw you in the streets
or sat down to edit my movie.
One night my producer came over
and fired me from my own project.

Today it is you, old friend,
editing the movie based on your life.
How in hell you got the job to be my replacement
is something I still hope you'll explain one day.
You're not even a filmmaker.

Anyway, it's been eighty-six days
since you took over post-production,
and I'm sure the movie is pretty much done. Even so,
I'm still waiting for the day you'll realize
this movie is based on your life.

# The Exorcism

O reasonably well-known driver
of the overrated light-blue convertible,
why do you bend machetes with your gray eyes?

There's stagefright in the way you take left turns.

When you pout, you spill dark thoughts in a pot.

I suspect you come from the line
of Baskervilles, post-dog.

—

Commission or no commission,
your paintings are full of spiders.

You measure poltergeists in your home
to predict the shrinking of St. Kilda's sheep.

A distracted Charon,
retired from Lethe,
always picks up the ashes of your diary.

—

A carillon rings in your head,
and you resent its sound
but enjoy the slow-boil resentment.

Even your mellow dog digs a good bone to pick.

—

I saw you on Brighton Beach the day after Christmas,
just as you came out of the water.

And yet we react in the same way
to the draft that makes toes curl
on time-warping winter evenings.

—


Forget where you're going.
Dress all in white,
close your eyes,
say something to the film crew outside your apartment.

There's no duel on your schedule tomorrow.
You'll be OK.

Look: a new diner has opened just down the block.

# Legendary Rock Star Coat

Good morning. It's good to see you back in my future.
I admit it, the clams in my brain lit up at the news
in their waves. The mold from the fountain
washed up nowhere. The half-eaten cardinal
hung like a candy cane from the bookstore awning,
blindsiding the cats: good morning, good morning.
I hear you're huggable again, the mayor even gave you a helicopter.
Still, I hope you don't mind me keeping my own
lantern. I may need that Mayflower vision.
Yes, yes, your marginalia did go a long way, but Jesus...

I've been status quo, thank you for not asking.
Brent geese are still my company,
and a few people still picket my vida loca,
but don't go full-orchestra about it. I'm all over
the news, widely read in the slaughterhouses.
I sustain the bookstore with my speed-reading impulses.
When fishermen go to bed, they dream of my karma.
Each morning I take a walk in front of the tavern,
look out at the sepia dunes and cry out, "Killer!"
I scrapple my sunlight. Wouldn't want it to go unfiltered.

So how will you get here? Your usual sugar donkey?
Can he carry the mass of your wine and your godhead?
Will you show up with Hessians? Will it be rainy
or boring? Will canaries go on strike? Lately,
as I redraft my memories, I lose corners.
The lawnmower people gave up hiding their horror
at carcasses popping up. The mountains still break.
They've built a house on the lot where we used to smirk,
but the wall with the shadow of your face is still there.
It's one of my most loaded places to visit.

Call me when you arrive. I'm sure you will.
For a few minutes let's think of each other as people.
Let's take a train to some very specific fissure
then bury our heads in each other's favorite confusion.
Your legendary rock star coat is safe in my labyrinth,
not hardened by foreshadowing.
Your eyes are still good and lost, don't worry.
When you're tired, feel free to peekaboo here.
We'll stare at death together and not rub tombs.
You don't need a permit to cry.

# One Night We Will No Longer Bear the Ocean

We danced in the streets, been at it for years,
but little had been worked out. You couldn't remember
the last complete sentence. The pool flickered with rotting apples.
I got angry but had my doubts. Love was as good a reason as any.
At one afterparty, the band was so good, we thought
we understood each other. We were shadows behind red curtains,
neither gathering dust nor leaning in for a kiss.
So that was it then: trees falling, and we plugged our ears.
Well, the trees don't care. They remember
the outdoor theater far better than the actors.
After many years, all that's left is a standalone door
in the garden. So much easier now to act our age.

# Trotskyist Cafeteria

Eventually you did get back home, though it took you hours.
　　Ripped clothes, sprains, stories for years.
Neighbors stared in noncommittal vectors. You never touched your hang
　　glider again
　　　　　until I poked it. And then
you guessed and guessed at how much I wanted to try it
　　while police kept pulling you over.


Sometimes you would hit an elk, sometimes read too many signs shrieking
　　on lawns, deflated alter egos, un-Snowden-ed emails.
Flew all the way to San Antonio to learn from a friend of a friend what your
　　ancestors
　　　　　had expected of you.
Allegorical woodsheds in childhood rooms. Canes become castles
　　become legal defense become clouds.


None are immune to this. Sometimes you tremble. Sometimes
　　the mountain slopes are late wounds. Sometimes
flashbacks to a one-night stand years ago creep like houseplants around your
　　favorite
　　　　　bed and breakfast,
the one you wrote to me about. It made me marvel
　　through tears at your changed handwriting,


at the way you looked across the faux Victorian room, at the eclipse in the
　　painting,
　　　at the latest sycophant fitting well with the velvet—
and everything derailed. Never look at mosquitos while crossing.
　　　　　Never think of childhood.
Never take credit for your prizefighting self-awareness
　　with pills sculpted into passed pawns.

It takes one block to get soaked after the late baseball game,
    a life to recover from hairballs of obscene analogies.
Much later, you understand. You hide your one-eighties
        in the proverbial rip currents.
Incidental spaetzle and the smell of fake red meat make it
    into too many heart-demoing memoirs.

I doubt either of us checks our diaries anymore:
    too many bees on sudden flowers,
too many ominous meadows across state lines. When I'm puzzled
        by love, your mind drifts
as remaining sunrays go undercover. We messed it up
    like dead people, like consolations.

A fabric of wandering eyes in Christmas tree form.
    Golden hair on the walls of the national gallery.
Scientists recommend a modicum of lewd behavior, but it's hard to find
        these days for all the death.
All libido in the rearview, we no longer get nervous.
    Sometimes our death stares are cozy.

Will I go look for you in the afterlife, echoing Brodsky snooping
    for Véronique's red velvet armchair in every
Trotskyist cafeteria in the city? Will the piano play itself after
        the estate sale?
Will there be diamonds? Always one more ferry leaving?
    Will I remember the street where you first looked past me?

Implication flickers in and out of dark matter, and I'm always one
    flipped page away from a Martian chronicle,
one rotted bovine carcass away from bagging the eel of meditation.
    For now, though,

most of these homes are uninhabited. Not even the dead are dumped
    behind the boarded-up windows.

A cartoon tells me I never lived here. A surgeon general's warning
    unpersons our books. The ghosts of Cerberuses past,
treasonous trees, screamed scrapbooks, bones rattling down
            the crumbling road—
so reassuring, so vacant in the regret. Our boxed dinners
    inedible for the parental advisory stickers.

Don't say I'm wrong. The squalls down Saint Lawrence River
    don't point to the room in which we felt nothing together.
All this traffic is just an excuse not to avert my eyes when I finally
            arrive on your porch
where my teacup still stands months later and your hand reaches
    into the bonfire seconds before it fades.

# The Gift

Patched up with tape and webs,
a hole in the wall reveals
a dusty Nabokov novel inside the shed,
your birthday present to me when I turned 22.

When the walls of the shed are knocked down,
dead butterflies will land on its cover.

I'll save it, of course.
I'll put it in my top drawer.
When we're both old,
I'll bring it to you
and suggest we read it together,

though you'll only say, "No, I didn't
give this to you. You must be
thinking of someone else."

# Regret

Later in life, we enter the neighborhood
bookstore and survey the new arrivals. We leaf
through the bestselling picture book about the Moon
that bites people. Down from the sky it swoops
and takes a chunk right out of you. A big chunk.
Sometimes a whole limb. A spleen. A heart.
The Moon is always big brother, and at the most
counterintuitive moment it will come down
and sink its teeth into you. Could happen to any of us.
Sometimes it dispenses life lessons. That
may be the most dispiriting part. The Moon
might put a bromide in your ear about
what to do if at first you don't succeed,
then bite your ear right off, or even your head.
Children of all ages must be telling each other
in hushed voices about the Moon's victims
and the shades of pink the trees acquire
while the Moon gently creeps. "Isn't this amazing?"
you say. "I wish *I* had thought of this.
This is the freshest thing I've seen in years!"
I cannot help but agree and notice how
your jawline, which used to fascinate me till morning,
reflects the Sun, except for the eclipses.

# To Remain Human

When the song ends and the light hits you, fall on the floor
and recall the way you laughed for hours the first time
I held you. I told the artist about your smile,
and he sketched the shadows under your eyes.

The last ice cream I bought you was left behind
on the bench for raccoons that never showed up.
And then the rain went on into the next month,
soaking the abstract paintings on the porch.

And all the cushions are covered with pictures of houses.
Humans spill out of their windows, roll down the slopes
and into the Sun. An eclipse is coming.
Gestures turn to elegy in the dark.

# Acknowledgments

The author is grateful to the editors of the following publications where these poems first appeared, sometimes in an earlier version:

*823 on High:* "Betrayal"

*Better Than Starbucks:* "Memoir"

*The Café Review:* "Your Windmills Can Set Down Their Fireworks," "Timor Mortis Conturbat Me"

*Cardinal Points:* "Frog Pond," "The Gift"

*CityLitRag:* "The Line Between Our Lanes"

*Gramma Poetry:* "Bedside Paperback," "The Car You Drove That Night Was Silver"

*Journal of New Jersey Poets:* "Eventually the Scenery Changed," "Previously Owned by God," "Key West," "Legendary Rock Star Coat"

*KGB Bar Online Literary Review:* "After," "I've Sat on This Perch for Decades, and Now It's Time to Get Up," "I Hope You're Wonderful," "To Remain Human"

*Lily Poetry Review:* "The Minimalist Muzak," "Sometimes Your Name Appears on Random Paintings"

*LiveMag:* "I Throw Boulders Out of My Window Sometimes"

*Local Knowledge:* "How to Keep Warm" (based on a map by Donald Zirilli)

*Milkweed Poetry:* "The Self-Conscious Gorgeousness of Sunsets"

*The New Yorker:* "The Exorcism"

*Nixes Mate Review:* "Coffins of the Living"

*Of Zoos:* "Never Come to Terms" (the original published version was co-authored with Emily Brandt; only my part of the poem is used in this book)

*One Art:* "Your Voice" (as "Her Voice"), "Inverness"

*Otoliths:* "Chicken"

*Plume:* "Regret"

*Posit:* "Everything Thrown Out Except for Their Eyes," "The Cedar Creek"

*PostMortem:* "Catching Up"

*Prelude:* "Marconi Seashore," "At the James Joyce House"

*The Rutherford Red Wheelbarrow:* "A Table for Two Scrapes the Floor," "God Under Your Bare Feet," "The Forgotten Years," "The Grass Highway," "Derangement"

*Sensitive Skin:* "I Held You Like a Pencil Drawing" (as "I Held Her Like a Pencil Drawing"), "For Here There Is No Place"

*Shot Glass Journal:* "Adorable"

*StatORec:* "At the Airport Hotel"

*upstreet:* "Anxiety," "One Night We Will No Longer Bear the Ocean"

*White Rabbit:* "Exhibition Match"

# About the Author

Anton Yakovlev's poetry chapbook *Chronos Dines Alone* (SurVision Books, 2018) won the James Tate Poetry Prize. He is also the author of *Ordinary Impalers* (Kelsay Books, 2017) and two prior chapbooks: *Neptune Court* (The Operating System, 2015) and *The Ghost of Grant Wood* (Finishing Line Press, 2015). His poems have appeared in *The New Yorker, The Hopkins Review, Plume, Reed Magazine, upstreet, Poetry Daily*, and elsewhere. His translations from Russian have appeared in *Exchanges, Circumference, On the Seawall, Lunch Ticket*, and *Yes Poetry*, among others. The bilingual volume *The Last Poet of the Village: Selected Poems by Sergei Yesenin Translated by Anton Yakovlev* came out from Sensitive Skin Books in 2019. Anton co-hosts the Carmine Street Metrics reading series in Manhattan and the Rutherford Red Wheelbarrow reading series in Rutherford, New Jersey. A graduate of Harvard University, he is a former education director at Bowery Poetry Club. He has also written and directed several short films.